UTOPIAN TRACE

UTOPIAN TRACE

AN ORAL PRESENTATION

BY

PETER LAMBORN WILSON

UTOPIAN TRACE: AN ORAL PRESENTATION

BY PETER LAMBORN WILSON

LOGOSOPHIA, LLC
90 Oteen Church Road
Asheville, NC 28805
www.logosophiabooks.com
logosophiabooks@gmail.com

Library of Congress-in-Publication Data
Wilson, Peter Lamborn
Utopian Trace: An Oral Presentation

ISBN 978-0-578-49110-3

Distributed by Small Press Distribution
Non-Fiction

Cover art: *The North American Phalanx*, circa 1847-55. Unknown artist. (Collection of Monmouth County Historical Association, Gift of the Bucklin Family, 1936.) Back cover: *Frederick Law Olmsted* by John Singer Sargent, 1895. (Photo by Krys Crimi, Biltmore Estate, Asheville, NC, public domain.)

Book design by Susan Yost

Bronze statue of Frederick Law Olmsted at the North Carolina Arboretum, created by Zenos Frudakis in 2016. (Photo by Krys Crimi.)

UTOPIAN TRAILS IN CENTRAL PARK

A RADIO SERMONETTE PRESENTED ON
WBAI-FM, 1991

THIS PAPER IS ABOUT FREDERICK LAW OLMSTED and the ideological background, the philosophical background, to his work on Central Park. And it's a paper especially for New Yorkers—I don't know whether in other cities they will find this of any interest, but we are all, I would assume Central Park fans—I know I have felt, had a chauvinistic feeling about Central Park for many years, I have always considered it one of the finest major urban parks in the world, in my experience. I was never interested before in the designer of the park, Frederick Law Olmsted. But, you will see as I read the paper how I cottoned on to exactly what a fascinating character he is. And if you can't say anything else about the man, he is a major benefactor of humanity. He gave us Central Park, Prospect Park, Riverside Park, he worked on Riverside Park, he worked on other parks all over the country from Boston to San Francisco, literally. He was one of the first people to suggest Yosemite as a national park, so he is also one of the fathers of the national park movement. He is altogether an admirable character. I would go so far as to call him a hero of the people. So, here is my exploration into Frederick Law Olmsted.

I call it "Utopian Trails in Central Park." And I begin with a quotation from Walter Benjamin, and his essay "Central Park."

The longing of the human being for a purer, more innocent, more spiritual experience than he has been granted necessarily seeks its warranty (unterpfand) *in nature.*

– Walter Benjamin, "Central Park"[1]

Now, oddly enough, the essay quoted here is *not* about Central Park. No one seems to know why Benjamin called a series of disjointed notes on Baudelaire and commodity culture "Central Park." Spencer, the translator of the essay, says it's because "these fragments constitute the key, or central clearing in the tangled mass of the never-published archives known as the Arcades Project,"[2] fully discussed in Susan Buck-Morss' wonderful book *The Dialectics of Seeing*. *[Which I have actually reviewed on this program.]*[3]

Elsewhere I've read that when Benjamin put this text together he was planning to escape to New York, and so bestowed the title in token of his hope. This seems even less likely. *[Parenthetically, I should add that before he was able to get to America, of course, he was hounded to suicide by the Nazis.]*

---

1   Benjamin, W. "Central Park," *Walter Benjamin: Selected Writings, Volume 4, 1938-1940*; Eiland, H., Jennings, M.W., Eds.; Belknap Press of Harvard University Press, 2003.

2   *Now at last in print: The Arcades Project,* Walter Benjamin, Howard Eiland and Kevin McLaughlin, translators. Belknap Press, 2002.

3   *The Dialectics of Seeing: Walter Benjamin and the Arcades Project,* Susan Buck-Morss. The MIT Press, 1990.

Actually, Central Park would have provided a perfect subject for Walter Benjamin, as a setting for his hero, the *flâneur*, or "aimless stroller," as an emblem of the emergence of commodity culture, as an echo or embedding of utopian dreams. Walter Benjamin loved Charles Fourier, both for his utopian socialism and his proto-surrealist *panache*. Did Benjamin know that Frederick Law Olmsted, the chief architect of Central Park, had been influenced by the wave of Fourierism that swept America in the 1840's and 50's? Had he guessed that Central Park was meant as an embodiment of this enthusiasm? As an homage to Walter Benjamin *and* Frederick Law Olmsted, I'd like to imagine what the essay "Central Park" might have been like if Benjamin had written it about Central Park.

Walter Benjamin in 1928. (Courtesy of the Walter Benjamin Archive, Akademie der Künste, Berlin.) Portrait of Charles Fourier by Samuel Perkins Gilmore. (Courtesy of University of Kentucky Special Collections.)

What would have impressed Benjamin about Frederick Law Olmsted in this, his first work of landscape architecture? The following essay, or "attempt," tries to guess at some of the insights Benjamin might have obtained during his first walk in an alternate reality where he had escaped Nazism and suicide, around Olmsted's masterpiece.

In Zen practice one speaks of "beginner's mind," the ease, freshness and grace of the first performance, the first plunge into meditation. We use the phrase "beginner's luck"—but luck is only part of it. Human beings are by nature already enlightened, but have forgotten it. The beginner sometimes recalls this state unconsciously, and thus *fully* in mind and body at the first moment of spiritual or artistic undertaking. Zeami, the great Zen theoretician of Noh theater, calls this quality "the first flower" and maintains that the perfection of Noh is already fully expressed in the movements of apprentice boy actors. Once this flower is lost it may take decades to recapture through art, so that the oldest performers eventually display a conscious blossoming of enlightened esthetic, a *last* flower.

As the Sufi poet Hafiz put it, "Love, which at first seemed so easy, has fallen into difficulties."

Central Park came out of Frederick Law Olmsted's beginner's mind. He had *no* credentials for the job he undertook with all the typical self-assurance of the Victorian-American gentleman amateur, other than a predilection for aimless mooching about in European parks. There were no parks in America then, not one.

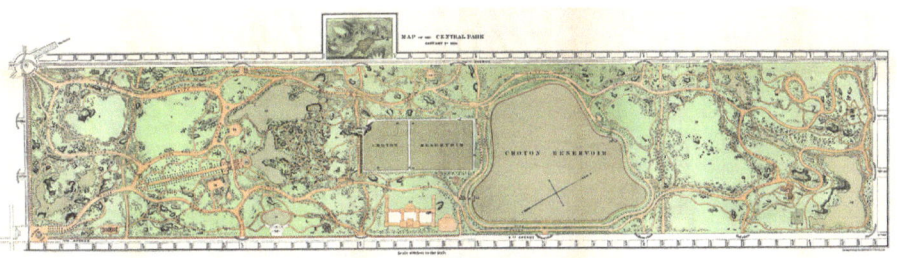

Vaux and Olmsted's 1870 map of Central park for the Thirteenth Annual Report of the Board of Commissioners of the Central Park. (Courtesy of Geographicus Rare Antique Maps.)

Olmsted had tried a bit of desultory farming financed by his generous and long-suffering father; first on the Connecticut seacoast, then on Staten Island. He grew pears, an interesting parallel with Fourier, who loved pears, and often used pear growing as an illustration of his schemes for attractive labor.

But Frederick Law Olmsted soon grew bored with the actuality of farming. It was fine in *theory*. He signed some of his earliest journalistic pieces as "farmer," or "American farmer." He was *great* on *theory*.

Eventually, he turned to full-time journalism. While staying at an inn in rural Connecticut, in order to work on some essay, he learned from a dinner companion that New York City had decided to build a park and that the job of architect had not yet been assigned. On an impulse, Olmsted decided to apply. He rounded up his most impressive literary friends to recommend him, including such prominent figures as William Cullen Bryant, who had, in fact, been the first to propose the park project, and the venerable Washington Irving, and the Fourierist newspaper man, Horace Greeley.

Horace Greeley around the time he printed Olmsted's articles in the New York Observer. (Photo by Matthew Brady, courtesy of Library of Congress, Prints and Photographs division.)

Olmsted got the job.

The city then, offered a two-thousand dollar award for a park design. Olmsted and his new partner, the English landscape gardener Calvert Vaux, entered the competition with a plan called "Greensward," and won.

So far in life Olmsted had failed at everything. He dropped out of college and flopped as a sailor, though he greatly enjoyed his one voyage to China. He had done poorly as a farmer, though he loved the land. And his journalism, though respected by the judicious few, failed to pay the rent.

No one, except Olmsted, had any reason to expect him to succeed in a profession that scarcely existed, in the face of New York City bureaucracy, graft and corruption, in a job so complex and vast. But Olmsted had found his *métier* at last. The year was 1857.

Two years earlier the American Fourierist movement had come to an official end with the closing of its longest surviving experiment, the North American Phalanx, in Red Bank, New Jersey. This last phalanstery once had scores of sibling communities, including Brook Farm, whose Transcendentalist, Fourierist luminaries were friends of Olmsted's. But the tide of Fourierism had past, giving rise to new enthusiasms in its wake. Three years earlier yet, in 1852, the North American Phalanx had still been firmly established, and Fourierism still the craze.

Olmsted, an aspiring journalist, visited the North American Phalanx and wrote a piece about it for Horace Greeley's *Daily Tribune*, always a good market for Fourieristic agitprop. Olmsted's piece grew out of a letter he wrote about the North American Pha-lanx, to an old friend, Charles Loring Brace. I'd like to quote the whole letter,[4] along with the notes [*or some of the notes, anyway*] appended by the editors of Olmsted's collected papers, in order to demonstrate Olmsted's personality, as well as his feelings about Fourierism.

Frederick Law Olmsted in 1850, two years before he visited the North American Phalanx. (Unknown attribution, courtesy of Wikimedia Commons.)

4   "To Charles Loring Brace, At the North American Phalanx: July 1852," *Frederick Law Olmsted: Writings on Landscape, Culture and Society,* Charles Beveridge, editor. Library of America, 2016, p. 45-55. The footnotes within this letter are adapted from the endnotes of this book. The only illustration original to this letter is Olmsted's drawing of the girl in a bloomer.

Charles Loring Brace in 1855 at age 29.

Dear Charley,

[I'm just going to read the whole thing; don't worry about details if you don't follow certain things. I'll try to explain the important ones as we come to them.]

Mr. and Mrs. Field, Rosa, Dr. Niedhard and myself were the party. Dr. Niedhard is an unusually sensible, reliable, good-hearted, stout, heavy, common-looking, democratic, socialistic, Christianic, German Homeopathic physician, standing high in this profession, & having a profitable practice in Philadelphia. Had seen your letters in Bulletin, not your book.[5] Was sorry not to see you & would be glad to do so when convenient for you.

The Navesink Highlands *[Which is the part of NJ that they're visiting.]* are a narrow range of hills extending down the shore, but little further than we went with Benny. *[Another friend.]* Then along their southern base there comes the Shrewsbury or Neversink River, and embouching into the *inlet* opposite the ocean house a few miles below our *peach-harbor*. *[He's talking about his farm on Staten Island.]* Going up this 7 miles or so to Redbank—a very beautiful country. The south shore flattish & rather marshy. North, hilly with beautiful slopes to the shore—on which are woods,

---

5   Brace's letters from Hungary were originally published in the *Philadelphia Bulletin*, and later in book form as *Hungary in 1851*.

orchards & cultivated fields—very charmingly mingled. Finer than Staten Island.

From Redbank we start for the phalanx by a *diligence*. [*A type of carriage.*] Country very pretty—sandy and sterile, but by marl & capital culture bearing fine crops. Hilly, well wooded & watered. Further you go, less pretty—more half cleared land, less diversity of surface &c.

About ten miles—you come to the domain—no indication of approach—woody country—large old brown mill—water & steam power, saw & grist &c. Enter a farm gate & by a good road through pretty wild wood 5o to 1oo rods to the phalanstery. No grounds— [*No gardens he means.*] an old barrack attached to a little old Dutch cottage, & back of this a few rods, a rather fine neat brown wood, hotel looking building. [*That was the famous phalanx itself.*]

THE NORTH AMERICAN PHALANSTERY.

We land on the piazza of it & enter a cold reception room. Plain, matted floor—engraving, head of Fourier & Swedenborg [*A lot of the settlers at the North American Phalanx were Swedenborgians, as well as followers of Fourier.*] & plaster angel & a vase or two. Visitors' register on table. Nobody in sight for some time and we *waiting*.

I am looking out of window & see from the aforesaid barrack a human being approaching. It is Horace Greeley in a bloomer. [*This is a joke. Horace Greeley was the editor of the Tribune, and although he was a political, or ideological ally of Olmsted's, they didn't get along too well. Olmsted liked to poke fun at him, as though he was rather a silly character. And a bloomer is the costume consisting of a short skirt over floppy trousers, which was invented by Amelia Bloomer, I think her name was, one of the most serious-minded of the female reformers of the 19th century who invented this feminist costume, called "bloomers," and they were at that time a fashion of the radical. If you were a radical woman you would wear bloomers. So he's making a joke at Horace Greeley's expense here. He's approached by this woman who he says looks like Horace Greeley in a bloomer.*] The same high expansive noble benevolent forehead & eye—rather withered in the sensual. The same floxy hair & a devil may care air about looks & a take it easy carriage & expression. She is between 30 & 50 & looks healthy & good in spite of the outrageous oddity.

Olmsted's drawing in the letter.   Amelia Bloomer in 1851.

She comes & salutes us mildly. Tells us most of Field's acquaintances are not here. (Spring,[6] for one, for your luck.) But others are brought, dinner ordered, & Mrs. Arnold,[7] as good a specimen of the best sort of New England little oldish woman as I ever saw. Mild, loving, earnest, simple, thin, and monstrously over-worked. She is our hostess & we are made guests—dine, and Field & I, with a young pair of Arnolds, look over the crops, the marl pit &c.

There are about 100 members & 50 visitors, children,

---

6   Marcus Spring, a cotton merchant and a major stockholder in the North American Phalanx.

7   Lydia Spring Arnold, married to Phalanx president George Arnold, and sister of Marcus Spring.

& probationers. No one can join until after a year's probation he or she is accepted by a majority vote. Visitors pay cost (same as members for dishes at table & $2 a week for profit, & 37¢ for rent. So it costs as a mere boarding-house $3 to 5 a week.) [*This was very cheap, even then.*]

The attention of the community has thus far been evidently given to merely financial success. They have evidently worked hard & constantly. And though from inexperience they made a good many errors at first and have had a great many peculiar difficulties, they have succeeded in *making it pay*. A great success. They have done little but in agriculture to make money by. And when you consider how hard it is to make a living by agriculture in general, [*Something Olmsted was learning to his cost.*] you will acknowledge they have shown a great advantage in the co-operative principle as applied to it.

They have, as I intimated, neglected anything else almost in the endeavor to make money. There has been little thought of beauty or moral or mental advancement. Education of the young has been forgotten in a great measure. There is surprisingly little concern for appearances. They all talk and act *naturally*, simply and unaffectedly. Evidently care little, too little, for the *world* outside. Pay but little attention to visitors and greatly love one-another.

They generally are strongly attached to the Phalanx, feel confident that it is the right way to live. Have enjoyed it & succeeded in their purposes in it much better than they had expected to. "I *wouldn't* leave for worlds." "Couldn't live any other way." "It is heaven compared to the life I had before," &c., we heard from different individuals.

It is considered a great privilege to be permitted to join them and they reject a great many. I can not tell what sort of people they were. Mostly New Englanders I should think—of various classes—the majority working people. Few or none independently wealthy. Whether any considerable number were actually mere laborers living from hand to mouth, uneducated and uncouth, I could not be satisfied. Some of the later ones were. Many of the old ones might have been and if so have been a good deal refined and civilized by the associative life.

If we compare their situation with that of an average of the agricultural class—laborers & all—even in the best of New England, it is a most *blessed* advance. They are better, in nearly all respects. And I don't see why, if such associations were common, and our "lowest class" (I mean poorest & least comfortable and least in the way of improvement moral & mental) of laborers could be drawn of their own will into it, they should not be in the same way advanced in every way. Put a *common-place* man (if a common-place man would choose to be so put) of our poorest Agricultural or Manufacturing laboring class into *such circumstances*, and it looks to me every way probable that he would be greatly elevated—be made a new man in a few years.

On the other hand take the average of our people of all classes including the wealthy and gay fashionable—including our merchants & shop-keep-ers & lawyers & ministers—and I think on the whole the influence of the system, if they would keep to it, would be favorable. They would live sensibly, be hap-pier & better.

If you take our most intelligent religious & cultivated sensible people, I think it would depend on individual character, on individual tastes. I half think (though my taste would say otherwise) it would be better for me. For you & J.H.O. & Field [*And other friends that he men-tions, he is talking to his friend Charles Brace.*] it would require a change, a good deal of a struggle, to come handsomely and profitably into it.

The long & short of it is [*Here is an important sen-tence.*] I am *more of a Fourierist* than before I visited the Experiment. The conglomeration of families even works better than I was willing to believe. Neverthe-less, I am not a Fourierist for myself: but for many, a large part of even an American community (peo-ple) I am. It wouldn't suit me—certainly not Field or J.H.O. But I think it would the majority. An Associa-tionist—a Socialist—I very decidedly more am than I was before I went to the Phalanx. The advantages of cooperation of labor are manifestly great. The sav-ing of labor immense. The cheapening of food, rent, &c., very great. It would make starvation, abundance. The advantages by making knowledge, intellectual & moral culture, and esthetic culture more easy—popu-lar—that is, the advantages by *democratizing* religion, refinement & information, I am inclined to think might be equally great among the *associated.* [*That is*

*to say the people who live in a phalanx are in an asso-
ciation.*] They are not at the N. A. Phalanx & yet are
manifest among some.

[*This deserves to be explained a little, it is hard to understand his writing. What he means is that the advantages of
"democratizing religion refinement and information" — in
other words of making it available to all classes equally
in the setting of a phalanx or a commune or an association — these advantages should be quite obvious among the
experimenters, the communitarians. He says he doesn't find
them to be so widespread at the North American Phalanx,
and yet they are manifest among some of the members. This
is a moderate criticism that he is giving here; that although
they're so successful as agriculturalists, he feels that on the
cultural level, they're not manifesting as much benefit as
they might in the Fourieristic system. This is an important
criticism to remember. Getting back to the letter…*]

Those who came there already refined, religious,
(moral at least) & highly intelligent may have suffered. I
saw no evidence that I know that they had, but I should
have thought they would. Because they had given
themselves up to too narrow ranges of thought—have
worked too hard to make the association succeed—or,
if you please, too hard for the benefit of others.

It is not, by any means, yet a well-organized &
arranged establishment. They are constantly improv-
ing—seeing errors and returning to do up matters
which in the haste of a struggle to get started were
overlooked. Yet they see an immense deal to be
attended and better arranged when they get time. Nor
are they *very* intelligent people or very refined and

genteel and of high ideals—*any of them*. There are lots of conveniences they might have—that would be necessary to the comfort of some wealthy people, even for you & I prospectively; that they know nothing about &, of course, care nothing about. They are not any of them *first class* people, or if so they have forgotten some of their 5th Avenue notions. I mean, *silver-forks* & such like—(napkins.)

One great thing they have succeeded in perfectly. In making *labor*, honorable. Mere *physical* labor they too much elevated, I think, but at any rate the "lowest" & most menial & disagreeable duties of civilized community are made really reputable & honorable. A man who spent a large part of his time in smoking & reading newspapers & talking and recreative employments only would feel ashamed of himself, [*I think Olmsted's thinking of himself here.*] would feel small & consider it a privilege to be allowed to black boots & sweep and milk for a part of the time.

It was in this way it would do me good to go there. No, not in making labor honorable, but in making idleness disagreeable & labor of all sorts (moderately) agreeable—in removing much that is disagreeable. Thus, I should hoe corn very comfortably, if I should have you, Charlie, in the next row to talk to about *the Schuss cogsslocken del Espelntatzellin*,[8] and should black my own shoes, & yours too if you paid me for it, if all that I needed to do was toss them into a hopper and turn the stop-cock and let on the steam.

---

8   Apparently Olmsted is parodying German philosophical language here with a nonsense phrase.

The whole of the work of the community is apportioned to different *groups*. Rather, first to series; as the "Agricultural Series," the "Domestic Series," "Live Stock Series," &c, & the series into groups. Thus, the Agricultural into the market garden, orchard, experimental, marling, &c., groups. The Domestic Series into — Cooking, Washing, Ironing, Baking, Dairy, &c.

On joining the community I enter my name on the list of whatever group I please — thus on the dairy, the orchard and the market-garden. I work an hour, say, at the churn, six hours at picking apples for market, and three at sorting potatoes. I am credited by so much on each of the groups' books. Each group votes on what the time of each member is worth. The ordinary "day's work" is from 90 cents to a dollar. [*That doesn't sound like much, but remember the rent is only five dollars a month.*]

The *chiefs* of all the groups of a Series hold conclaves with the "chief of the series" & arrange matters for the series. The series chiefs also meet under a head chief or *chief of the phalanx* & legislate on matters of more general character.

A man works at anything he finds himself suitable for. Many are members of a good many groups. If a man does not work with any group with which he is registered within two months, he is considered to have left it, &c. If a man only works occasionally, irregularly, his time is valued at a lower figure.

The dining room is much like that of a first class hotel — spacious & neat & comfortable. Tables arranged as in an eating-house, but large enough for perhaps a dozen to each. The *carte* [*Or menu.*] of each meal lies on the table (*carte du jour*) with the prices (cost) of the dishes, which as you know are very low. But every little item counts. Bread 1 cent, butter a ½ cent or 1 cent, plate of ros' beef, 3 cents, &c. Ice cream "*a la français*" — a big saucer full, 2 cents. The cost varies with the season. During drought & short pasture, buttercakes are graduated in stamping a little smaller, &c.

The main residential building of the North American Phalanx in 1972, a few months before it burned to the ground. (Courtesy Library of Congress, Prints and Photographs Division.)

The waiters are the prettiest & most refined and graceful young ladies of the community mainly— some of the "most respectable" young fellows, too. You are introduced to the waitress of your table.

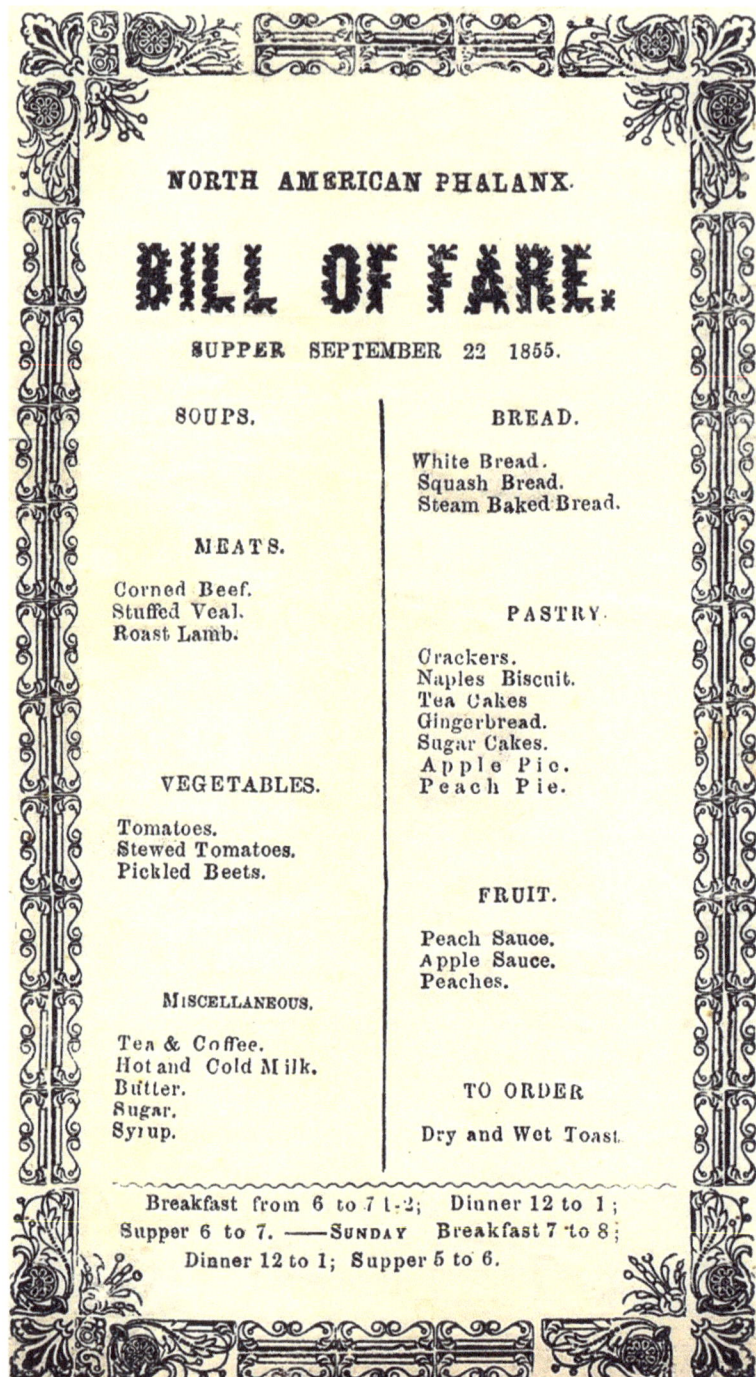

NORTH AMERICAN PHALANX.

BILL OF FARE.

SUPPER SEPTEMBER 22 1855.

SOUPS.

BREAD.

White Bread.
Squash Bread.
Steam Baked Bread.

MEATS.

Corned Beef.
Stuffed Veal.
Roast Lamb.

PASTRY.

Crackers.
Naples Biscuit.
Tea Cakes
Gingerbread.
Sugar Cakes.
Apple Pie.
Peach Pie.

VEGETABLES.

Tomatoes.
Stewed Tomatoes.
Pickled Beets.

FRUIT.

Peach Sauce.
Apple Sauce.
Peaches.

MISCELLANEOUS.

Tea & Coffee.
Hot and Cold Milk.
Butter.
Sugar.
Syrup.

TO ORDER

Dry and Wet Toast.

Breakfast from 6 to 7 1-2; Dinner 12 to 1;
Supper 6 to 7. —— SUNDAY Breakfast 7 to 8;
Dinner 12 to 1; Supper 5 to 6.

Miss Mundy mine was, a very good-looking, lady-like young woman, intelligent accomplished & well informed — dressed with great taste. It was odd enough & not altogether agreeable to hold a conversation with her upon *social* topics in which she showed a philosophical mind and a cultivated and refined judgement, she bending over my shoulder. She takes part in the general conversation of the table, but comes & goes as there is occasion. Is a very good waiter indeed — clean, sweet, and good-natured.

Why do all the best of the young people choose to be waiters & so to be deprived of the social enjoyment of the meals with their friends in a great measure? They all dine to-gether afterwards, and as they *are* the *best*, it is a privilege to dine with them — of course to wait with them. If it was not, they would be paid the best — (or should be.) So the most cultivated of the men are *attached* to the domestic groups (more or less — they generally also attach themselves to some of the out-door-exercising groups as well.) The chief of the series is a French physician. There are other foreigners, fine-looking gentlemen, also in it and the waiters, head waiters, carvers, &c.

There is one I must speak of particularly. He was the son of a wealthy, aristocratic family. Brought up in style; "got religion," became an Episcopal clergyman, was eloquent & much beloved & esteemed. Had a country church with a salary of $1,000. Didn't see that he was doing good. Worried & fretted & studied & prayed & fasted. Concluded the system was wrong & he was not sincere. Gave it up sick of life. Wandered & wasted.

Accidentally came hither. Stayed a week. And one night ran out & threw up his hat & declared the problem was solved. Here was a Christianity as was a Christianity & a church as was a church. Threw off his black coat & asked leave to work. Got tremendously tired, feverish, &c. Found it wouldn't do. But was determined to work with his hands—"in labor is prayer."—& went into domestic series. And we were introduced to him, a fine, sad, quiet gentlemanly fellow—*peeling potatoes*.

N.B. Nobody blushes or boasts or seems to consider such employments at all to be kept in the dark or anything less of a regular thing than taking off their clothes for themselves when they go to bed. The fact is they have reconstructed a world for themselves & have forgotten the ways of the world *outside*.

Five Points, New York City. Engraving from a painting by George Catlin in 1827. (Courtesy of Museum of the City of New York, Print Archives.)

I must tell you something of Mr. Arnold's history. He was a merchant in N.Y. greatly interested in Five

Point philanthropies. [*That means working, doing good in the slums of New York, the old Five Point district, which was the toughest part of town in those days.*] Gave himself much up to them—so too his wife. Both Massachusetts saints. He was finally so much interested in his reforming labors that he gave his whole time to them & the Unitarians made him *minister at large* with a roving commission much such as you would like.

He then threw himself into it. Gave himself to the work—until he got perfectly sickened, disgusted, and overwhelmed. With large means & doing nothing else, he found it was stopping leaks in a rotten ship. The more you stop the breech up, the more it was *widened*. Had a conviction much like that of the Episcopal clergyman that the system was wrong, that the so-called Church of Christ was wrong. That it was not Christianity he was preaching—that Christians did not love-one-another, &c., &c., &c.

Went to the West and found the most solitary place he could & there lived hermit-like with his family for several years. His wife says, it was the greatest relief & happiness to her to feel that there they could do others but *little* harm & others could do them but *little*.

While so situated, Mr. Spring (his wife's brother) went to Europe with * Fuller— ⁹ & while gone certain Fourierite periodicals that he had taken were sent to him (Arnold). He did not like them, but read them. So did his wife, until after a year both suddenly found each-other converted. They came to the Phalanx &

---

9   Author Sarah Margaret Fuller, who signed her pieces in the *New York Daily Tribune* with an asterisk.

are fully convinced that it must be this way only that the kingdom shall come.

The arrangement of the dormitories is much like that of a hotel; a large number of small bed-rooms for single parties and suites of rooms for families. There are three or four tenements adjoining the main-house, built into it like a *block* with no communication with it or with each other except by a gallery in the rear to enable the inmates to go to the dining-hall or the work rooms (kitchen &c.) dry shod. There is also one entirely detached cottage.

These families could have their meals sent to them (by some additional payment) but in fact none do — all preferring the common refectory. Here families have their usual tables separate from others if they choose. Families separate, though, a good deal. Husband & wife & the younger children generally together, but the older children "follow their attractions." That is, being generally *engaged* as soon as they are big enough, they sit with their espoused.

In the evening from supper till 10 o'clock or later there was a good deal of recreation, walking parties, rowing parties, dancing & music. There are 6 pianos in the establishment & several guitars, &c. There was a music teacher & a French teacher. Also one of the French refugees teaches fencing & dancing, &c. But recreation of this sort was not *general*. The less cultivated however spent the evening much more elevatingly than most country people do — in conversation & discussions. There is very little reading done.

Most of the young ladies and some of the older men dressed à la Bloomer, generally not very tastefully. [*You see some of the men actually wore these skirts too.*] Some appeared to much greater advantage when so than in long skirts. A graceful *action* was much more graceful and gratifying when the movement of the leg could be seen. Some were very short skirted. Usually the kilt reached an inch or two below the knee, or enough to reach over it in sitting. Not always though. There was the most perfect natural propriety & good sense among them all. The Bloomer has been naturalized, and in an hour you are as accustomed to it as you would be in China. It is "all right." Many who wore Bloomer in A.M. were in "evening dresses" later. Some appeared better & some worse for the change.

As to creeds, the majority are Swedenborgians, but there is nothing peculiar to the community. I should think persons of all the great nominally Christian churches from Catholics to Unitarians, or rationalists.

The very shortest Bloomer had me by the button sitting under the trees for half the evening telling me of her Spiritual Supping experience. She had had, during two months, frequent intercourse with her father who died eight years ago while she was a child, & received most delightful words from, and practical advice and assistance. [*We are talking about Spiritualism here.*] She believed it all as fully as she did or could anything not absolutely tangible. She recognized the influence of spirits constantly upon her as she did heat & light. It was a regular thing. Thought there was much humbug. Foxes & Fishes were imposters.

[Those were the Fox sisters and another famous Spiritualist called Fish.] Others fools—self deceived. Her yarn didn't amount to much. She was a person that would easily be imposed upon. *[I like this anecdote because it shows it was just like the hippy communes of the 60's, you meet some serious reformers; you meet some flighty person who's having spiritual séances, you know, it's very 1960's the whole thing.]*

I have been, since last sheet, reading *Tribune* of Saturday (23rd..) If you haven't it's worth it—on Spiritual Manifestations & the *Shekinah* article on Judge Edmonds.[10] And I add a little more.

She was convinced or held her faith entirely from the *moral* evidence—the general character of the communications she had received. First, though, she was startled by receiving answers to questions and suggestions in her own mind which she had not uttered or expressed in any way. As for material manifestations, she had certainly seen tables lifted and taken across a room. She had stood on a table and had been moved gently and steadily across the room & back to the exact spots on the carpet that the legs occupied before—no person being near the table, at 4 o'clock P.M., open daylight. It was in Massachusetts last spring or winter. The table was moved at her request to give evidence of the ability of the spirits to exercise material agency. Was guided as she directed, &c. As I said, she was the sort of person that would be easily imposed upon and be run away with by her

---

10 The article shared the experiences of New York Supreme Court Justice John Worth Edmonds, who believed that his deceased wife was attempting to communicate with him.

own imagination. Nevertheless, her facts & her faith impressed me with a little more respect for the matter.

As to the people of the community in general, I have a strong respect for them as hard-working, earnest, unselfish livers in the faith of a higher life for man on earth as well as "above." There were fewer odd characters than I should have expected to find. Generally, there was much simplicity and self-containedness among them. I think they are living devoutly & more in accordance with the principles of Christ—*among themselves*—than any equal number of persons I ever saw living in the usual neighborhood intercourse together.

There is a certain class that they very much need to have associated with them. I could not help wishing Charles Elliott[11] had joined them. Believing a good deal in their principles as I believe he does, he would have been exceedingly useful to them. They much need mechanics, but I think it is the fault of their theory that they do not have them. Their success without them is the more wonderful. I believe they have only one carpenter & a watch maker, or some such nearly useless thing to them. Having to pay high, of course, for all the mechanics brought to do work for them from a distance.

What they need for improvement as a community of moral creatures is more attention to the intellectual. They want an *Educational Series* very much. They have no fit teacher—a Frenchman for want of a better

11 Charles Wyllys Elliott, landscape horticulturalist and member of the Board of Commissioners of Central Park, was the person who suggested to Olmsted to apply for the position of park superintendent.

acts as schoolmaster to the fry. But there is no proper nursery department & the children, & not the children alone, are growing without any proper discipline of mind. A rum set one would think they would make. But I must confess those who are breaking into manhood and especially into womanhood tell well for the system. They are young *ladies* & young *gentlemen*. Naturally and without effort or consciousness, so.

You had better go there next fall. I'll go with you. Mr. Arnold was sorry you didn't come with us. And others would be glad to see you. If you could give them a lecture on Hungary they would be gratified. Hadn't you better get one up—with some reference to present position of things? Remodel your old one a little. I told them you would come bye & bye.

If we can make a boating-party for several days it will be pleasant in peach season—*October* rather too late. Charles Elliott ought to go with us. Be valuable to him as a market gardener.

All the folks here. Nothing of importance. Beckwith not yet bought. In a fortnight I may leave home for a little while.

Yours Affectionately,
Fred.

P.S. I have condensed this for the Tribune.[12] Told them if they didn't want to print it to direct to you & you would get it at the office.

---

12 "The Phalanstery and the Phalansterians. By an Outsider," *New York Daily Tribune*, June 29, 1852, under the pseudonym "An American Farmer."

[But in fact the Tribune did publish a version of this, I presume without the crack about Horace Greeley in a bloomer. So that's Olmsted's letter about Fourierism. You can see he is not a convinced Fourierist, but that he's very very sympathetic. But this was the point I wanted to make. I thought it was a very interesting account of a visit to an 1840's hippy commune. There's not much first hand information on the North American Phalanx. As Olmsted pointed out, most of the people there were not intellectuals, and not a lot of reminiscences and narratives, or letters came out of the North American Phalanx. So this is a very valuable document.]

I first found mention of this text in Carl Guarneri's definitive study of the American Fourierist movement *The Utopian Alternative: Fourierism in Nineteenth Century America*. In order to demonstrate my debt to Guarneri, who I believe was the first to propose Central Park as a Fourierist experiment, I will quote at length from this book.

The work of America's premier landscape architect and park designer, Frederick Law Olmsted, shows Fourierism's subtle influence on later shapers of the urban environment. As a gentleman farmer outside New York City, Olmsted became acquainted with Fourieristic ideas in the 1840s through his friends Greeley, Godwin and Marcus Spring. *[Spring is referred to in the letter.]* On his tour of English farms and cities in 1850, he met the British Fourierist Hugh Dougherty, *[Who translated Fourier's Passions of the Human Soul into English.]* and after his return he stepped up contacts with the Associationist movement. In 1852 he penned a series of appreciative articles on the North American Phalanx, *[I'm not sure what he means by "series"—I've only found one.*] based on visits there, praising its "advantages of cooperation of labor," "united household of families," and its diffusion of "moral…and aesthetic culture." Olmsted was a frequent guest at Marcus Spring's Raritan Bay Union [*Another phalanx.*] and he advised Victor Considérant on the location of his Texas colony. [*Considérant was Fourier's main French disciple who had to flee Paris after 1848, and went to Texas to try and start a phalanx. And Olmsted knew Texas quite well, and advised Considérant on a place to settle.*] Though Olmsted never joined a phalanx or Fourierist club, he provided warm public testimonials to the Associationist movement.

The Raritan Bay Community in Perth Amboy, New Jersey in 1858. It ran from 1853-60, after which it became the Eagleswood Military Academy. (Courtesy of the New Jersey Historical Society.)

Long after Fourierism disappeared as a distinguishable movement, [*Actually not that long—five years later.*] Olmsted translated some of its key ideals into America's largest and most important public parks. In New York's Central Park and elsewhere, Olmsted's plans reflected the Fourierist ideal of a harmonious counterpoint of city and country environments; the Fourierists' belief in varied group recreation as a basic human need; and their conviction that society had a duty to provide public facilities for communal activities. As an outdoor analogue to the phalanstery, the municipal park was a public meeting ground where social classes mingled, and a communal spirit replaced selfish individualism. In 1870, in his most concise statement of the social ideal of city planning, Olmsted described Central Park and Brooklyn's Prospect Park as "the only places in those...cities where... you will find a large body of Christians coming together, ...all classes largely represented, with a common purpose, not at all intellectual, competitive with none, disposing to jealousy or spiritual or intellectual pride toward none, each individual adding by his mere presence to the pleasure of all others, all helping to the greater happiness of each." Like public transit, sewers, and gas and water works, municipal parks demonstrated that city life was evolving from wasteful individualism toward efficient collective control of resources and technology. Olmsted found in antebellum Fourierism an ideal of social interdependence and a theory of historical development to give landscape architecture its largest meaning. Yet, because his parks were meant to mitigate the effects of urban fragmentation and competition rather than overturn the society that produced them, they exemplify the evolution of utopian ideals into institutional reform in the late nineteenth century.[13] [*Actually, this is the theme of my paper.*]

There is no evidence in any of this to show that Olmsted had actually read Fourier. But, then, neither had most American Fourierists. Albert Brisbane and the other leaders of the movement (including Greeley here.) boiled down and filtered the writings of the founder, eliminating his orgiastic sexuality, his enthusiasm for wine and food—gastrosophy, the "wisdom of food"—his anti-Christianity, his occultism, his hatred of civilization and philosophy, his praise of luxury and

13 *The Utopian Alternative: Fourierism in Nineteenth Century America*, Carl J. Guarneri. Cornell University Press, 1994, p. 399-400.

sensual pleasure, his astounding cosmological visions, even his risqué humor, and presented only his theories of society and labor.

It is interesting to note that Olmsted's criticisms of the North American Phalanx strike points which Fourier himself would have emphasized had he lived to see what a hash the Americans made of his theories. Fourier too would have disliked the neglected and shabby grounds. Beauty was not an extra, or a luxury in the usual sense of the word, but a necessity. There could exist no true phalanx without this minimal requirement. Fourier would have denounced the absence of an educational series, and of course he would have hated the food, the tea-totalitarianism, the dullness, and asexuality.

Like Olmsted, he would have protested, that not even a gentleman could live like this, much less the true harmonian human, whose need for luxury, excess and brilliance outshines the mere gentleman's taste as a star outshines a candle. The democratization of spirituality, manners and culture which Olmsted envisioned as the true goal of a phalanx meant as much to Fourier as the doctrine of attractive labor. Indeed, labor could never be attractive if it were not integrated with a life of art, music, good cheer, profound pleasure, love, and divine enthusiasm. Olmsted speaks wistfully of "making aesthetic culture more easy, or popular." This supremely Fourieristic goal had been neglected at the North American Phalanx. Five years later Olmsted was to make it the underlying philosophy of his design for Central Park.

Olmsted, at least as a younger man, was a radical. He ran guns to the Kansas Free Soil guerillas. [*The anti-slavery fighters in Kansas.*] And involved himself deeply in the attempts of German revolutionaries to found utopian communities in Texas. Olmsted was also a conservative. He possessed a Confucian sense of spontaneous propriety. He admired the Chinese above all for their graceful manners, and a sense of duty—duty to culture, duty to the poor, duty to be *cheerful*.

If Central Park flowed from his beginner's mind, still, he was no naïve instinctual medium for the muses. He possessed a philosophy, an idea about what a park *should* be. In this idea, his radical and conservative natures were alchemically joined and harmonized. His idea served both impulses.

"Men of literary taste or clerical habit…are always apt to overlook the working-classes, and to confine the records they make of their own times, in a great degree, to the habits and fortunes of their own associates or to those of people of superior rank to themselves. The dumb masses have often been so lost in this shadow of egotism, that, in later days, it has been impossible to discern the very real influence their character and condition have had on the fortune and fate of the nations."[14] [*This is from the Olmsted biography by Laura Roper, so that a bit of her writing is in here too. She says:*]

Inspecting a splendidly maintained Welsh castle set in a beautiful park, Olmsted was enraptured by the elegance and taste of the life it typified. But his immediate second thought was: "Is it right and best that this should be for

14 *F.L.O.: A Biography of Frederick Law Olmsted*, Laura Wood Roper. The Johns Hopkins University Press, 1983, p. xiv.

the few, the very few of us, when for many of the rest of us there must be but bare walls, tile floors, and every thing besides harshly screaming scrabble for life?" And his third thought was, "Whether in this 19th century of the carpenter's son, and first of vulgar, whistling, snorting, rattling, roaring locomotives, new-world steamers, and submarine telegraphs; penny newspapers, free schools, and working-men's lyceums, this still, soft atmosphere of elegant age was exactly the most favorable for the production of thorough, sound influential manhood[15]…"

The key to the answer to this question is the park, the "Garden Republic" as Olmsted called it. He approved of a journalist who wrote of Central Park's "moral influence:" its success both as a work of art, and as an experiment on the people, and our own democratic institutions. The journalist said he understood the "politico-moral aspects" of the work. I should note, by the way, the term "moral" was not used in the 19th century to refer to some narrower range of meanings as the word now connotes. True, Fourier used the term like Nietzsche much later, in an abusive sense, but for writers of English, it includes broad ethical and social implications. In this sense both Fourier and Nietzsche had moral philosophies. *[In other words, when Olmsted used the word "moral" a lot, you shouldn't think of him as some kind of Puritan or something. In fact, he was far from it, he was pretty anti-Christian himself.]*

Olmsted referred to his highest idea as communica-tiveness, a term resonant with Fourieristic overtones. In describing his later experiences as a manager of a

15 Roper, p. 69.

gold mine in California, he defined this term almost as something beyond good and evil. He wrote:

> I come to the conclusion that the highest point on my scale can only be met by the man who possesses a combination of qualities which fit him to serve others, and to be served by others in the most intimate, complete, and extended degree imaginable. Shall we call it communicativeness? Then I find not merely less of a community, but less possibility of a community, or communicativeness, here [*In California.*] among my neighbors of all kinds than in any other equal body of men I ever saw. And the white men, the Englishmen, the Germans and other civilized men do not possess it often in as high a degree as the Mexicans, Chinese and Negroes—nor do the good men always possess as much of it as the rogues, the wild fellows.[16]

Olmsted believed that Central Park succeeded in the long run because "the heart of the people was with us and was kept with us."

Laura Roper writes:

> Olmsted, trying some years later to explain the accelerating strength of the American park movement at this time, thought he detected another, more basic motive: society's instinct of self-preservation.
>
> "Parks have plainly not come as the direct result of any of the great inventions or discoveries of the century. They are not, with us, simply an improvement on what we had before, growing out of a general advance of the arts applicable to them. It is not evident that the movement was taken up in any country from any other, however it may have influenced or accelerated. It did not run like a fashion. It would seem rather to have been a common, spontaneous movement of

---

16 Roper, p. 253.

that sort which we conveniently refer to as the 'Genius of Civilization.'...

Why this great development of interest in the natural landscape and all that pertains to it; to the art and the literature of it?"

The final answer, he thought, lay in the first and strongest of instincts: "Considering that it has occurred simultaneously with a great enlargement of towns and development of urban habits, is it not reasonable to regard it as a self-preserving instinct of civilization?"

Olmsted did not hate cities or think them fatal to civilization; he hated barbarism. It was principally in cities and well-regulated suburbs, he recognized, that many of the graces of civilization can be enjoyed: effective and effortless sanitary arrangements; goods and physical comforts, attainable in the country only by hard work; services to match every need; and leisure, society, recreation, and intellectual pleasures. But cities, growing ever larger, becoming ever more crowded, were also hotbeds of misery, vice, crime, and disease. Moreover, they tended, Olmsted believed, to breed among their inhabitants not only physical ills, but a callous habit of mind. One could not walk down a crowded street without constantly having to watch, to foresee, and to guard against the movements of others. "This involves a consideration of their intentions, a calculation of their strength and weakness, which is not so much for their benefit as our own. Our minds are thus brought into close dealing with other minds without any friendly flowing toward them." City dwellers, every day of their lives, "have seen thousands of their fellow men, have met them face to face, and yet, have had no experience of anything in common with them." This lack of communicativeness, as he called it, was to Olmsted the very essence of barbarism.

A park had a powerful countervailing influence. It not only helped to offset the physical ill effects of the city's congestion, hurry, and noise; it not only exerted on the minds of individual beholders a soothing and edifying effect; it also gave to people of all classes the opportunity to meet and mingle in casual friendliness, to enjoy the same circumstances side by side, yet independently, and to come together "with a common purpose, not at all intellectual, competitive with none, disposing to jealousy and spiritual or intellectual pride toward none, each individual adding by his mere presence to the pleasure of all others, all helping to the greater happiness of each." Parks stimulated, he thought, that sense of communicativeness that was the intrinsic quality of civilization; and American society, in an instinctive effort of self-preservation, was cultivating in its urban soil their civilizing influence [*That is, of parks.*] to counteract the barbarizing tendencies indigenous to the same's soil.[17] [*Long quote from Laura Roper in which she's basically boiling down Olmsted's ideas.*]

Like all great works of art, the exact genesis of Central Park's realization begins and remains in mystery.

"The sum is that I put into Central Park, and so did [*Calvert*] Vaux and the others, a degree of devotion that no greed and no selfish ambition would have induced. Why—how I came to—does not concern the public. It is not necessary that you should fully understand it. The fact is, that there was an artistic devotion in the early Central Park work such as a political work, short of war, seldom engages, and something of this fact it may be well the public should recognize."[18]

Laura Roper suggests that the psychological origins of Olmsted's passion for the park must have revolved around the recent death of his beloved younger brother, who had been his closest intimate. He later

---

17 Roper, p. 318-19.

18 Roper, p. 452.

married his brother's widow, but at the time, his love life was a failure, as were his abortive careers as farmer and journalist. Yet Olmsted clearly understood that the park added up to more than the sum of its parts, origins, roots, elements. The park opened onto a vista that transcended the artifice, compromise, and Victorian values which engendered it. The park was liminal— light, shade, color, texture, odor, the sensual elements of life so vital in Fourier's doctrine here alchemically mix and transmute into a single, precise, yet indefinable authenticity.

The park has a kind of satori, a kind of mystical enlightenment to it, its own and proper moment of realization. Here one enters the grounds of a great phalanstery, and even though the phalanstery itself is absent, the grounds are present, and thus constitute an opening onto another world, an alternate reality where Fourier's ideas somehow succeeded in transforming all of society and nature. Central Park exists simultaneously in our world and in utopia. Or to put it another way, Central Park constitutes a *trace* of that world within our world, a prolongation, a benign haunting.

We don't know much about Fourier's exact tastes in landscape. The design for a phalanstery by Victor Considérant which appears repeatedly in Fourierist literature reveals 18th century formal tastes, a democratic Versailles, strong on covered arcades—an obsession of Fourier's and also of Walter Benjamin's. Presumably the immediate grounds work would also have been carried out in the formal French style, but Fourier also envisioned a varied surrounding landscape, including farmland, orchards and woods. Central Park, too, has a formal center, The Mall and Bethesda Fountain, surrounded by a more naturalistic greensward.

Skizze eines Phalanx=Gebäudes (**Phalanstère**).

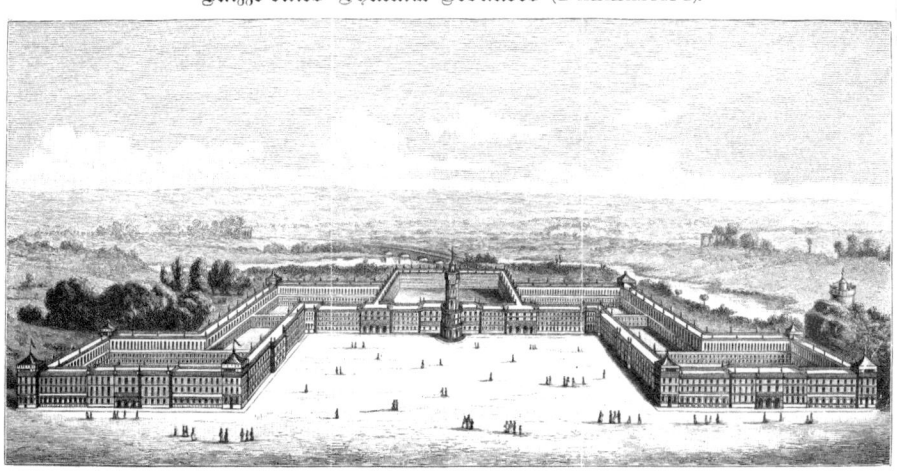

Charles Fourier's phalanstery design from a nineteenth century German wood engraving. (Courtesy Granger Historical Picture Archive.)

Fourier's attitude towards nature and landscape was both ecological and progressive. *[Of course these are terms he would not have used, they're modern terms.]* That is, he understood that the synergetic sum of the parts, or harmony, in a balanced environment constitute more than mere addition, but rather an astonishing multiplication, or even calculus—the so-called calculus of passion—which Fourier expressed with hyperbolic numero-mania. He measured things in millions, especially happiness and wealth.

But harmony was to come about through human engineering of ecology and landscape. In one memorable passage Fourier advocates *painting mountains* to achieve certain cosmico-social effects. His ideal world was neither wilderness nor city, but precisely: a park, an arboretum, set with pavilions and palaces, bucolic, but elegant. In such a setting, he believed, nature itself would spontaneously and very quickly undergo essential transformations. The climate would change, the seas would literally turn to lemonade, as in the folk utopia "Big Rock Candy Mountain." And such dangerous creatures as lions and sharks would be transmuted into friendly and useful anti-lions and anti-sharks. Nature as it *should* be.

On one level nature and culture present a dichotomy to human awareness. Even the most archaic hunter-gatherers experience a nostalgia for lost contact with nature, for a lost authenticity, which emblematizes itself for them *as* nature. Hence the spiritual world view once called totemism. A term, which still, I believe holds some value, and should not be discarded.

The masque, ritual or psychedelic drug, these are channels or initiatic media through which the tribe maintains one foot in culture, while stepping *out* into wildness. Or wilderness.

The totem in this sense provides a border, or fence between us and it, between culture and nature. This nexus space, or borderland and its artifacts are uncanny and witchy, suffused with *manna*. They are numinous. [*This is a numinous space in other words.*] The park itself is such a borderland, a numinous place, and here, we begin to approach the image of the park as *paradise*, derived from the Persian word for garden, *firdaus*, the space, or higher level in which nature and culture are reconciled or harmonized, *totemic space*.

Seventeenth century Persian garden carpet, depicting the rivers, trees and animals of paradise, detail. ("Wagner" Garden Carpet, courtesy of Glasgow Museums, Burrell Collection.)

Nothing in fact could be more utopian than a park. For the majority of human cultures have symbolized their golden age or paradise as a garden or parkland. The original "no-place" place, *utopos* in Greek. The image of nature perfected through divine humanity, but lost in time. Pure place, as yet unrecovered, but foreshadowed in the art of gardening.

Olmsted and Vaux worked mentally on their evolving landscape by taking long walks through the park
site and over its still-barren grounds *in the moonlight*.
Some say because they were too busy by day, others
however, because they wanted a certain *effect*. The
park as nocturne, so to speak.

Jacob Wray Mould at the Bethesda Terrace staircase under construction, 1862.
(Photo by Victor Provost, courtesy of the George Eastman Museum.)

Here the mid-19th century fad for things Moorish seems significant. Washington Irving, Olmsted's

patron, started it with his *Tales of the Alhambra*. [*By the way, a wonderful book if you've never read it.*] For Moorish projects Olmsted and Vaux hired the eccentric "ugly and uncouth but very clever J. Wray Mould, architect and universal genius."[19] The unjustly neglected Mould had actually traveled in the near east and had assisted Owen Jones in the preparation of his monumental study of the Alhambra. "Mould became deeply imbued with the spirit of Islamic architecture and applied its elegant proportions, lavish conventionalized ornament and colorful tile work to the enrichment of the Central Park Terrace and Arcade." [*It's a quote from a little pamphlet called* The Men Who Made Central Park *by M. M. Graff.*][20]

Thus, Central Park is meant in part as a reflection of the Alhambra and its garden palace, the Generalife in Granada, in Spain, which in turn were meant as reflections of paradise, the earthly paradise of "water, green things and a beautiful face," as the prophet Mohammed is supposed to have said. If heaven is a *city* for Christianity, it is a *garden* for Islam.

This aspect of Islam appealed to 19th century Romantics, just as Islam in general appealed to a certain anti-Christian free-thinking rationalist 19th century tendency. Olmsted harbored a strong dislike for organized Christianity, but he was certainly a nature mystic in the typical American vein. In short, he was both a rationalist and a Romantic.

---

19 Observation by George Templeton Strong, secretary of the Sanitary Commission, in *The Men Who Made Central Park*, M. M. Graff. Greensward Foundation, 1982, p. 20.

20 Graff. p.21.

Violin player busking below Bethesda Terrace. (Courtesy of Paul Lowry and Creative Commons.)

Early morning under the Moorish influenced Bethesda Terrace. (Photo courtesy of Francisco Diez and Creative Commons.)

Another component of Victorian American taste demanded the Gothic for its fulfillment. Olmsted and Vaux harbored no perverse attachment to the excesses of Gothic revival, but the mysterious nature of the park demanded a few touches, such as the now-vanished "Hermit's Cave" in the Ramble, [*Try to find that. It would be a nice project.*] and most notably the Gothic gem of the Belvedere Castle. The shape of the tower says "huge," but in fact is quite tiny, hence the eye is deceived on viewing it with a *trompe l'oeil* sensation of standing in a landscape much bigger than it really is.

Ramble Cave, Central Park in 1863 before it was sealed around 1930. (Courtesy of the The Miriam and Ira D. Wallach Division of Art, Prints and Photographs: Photography Collection, The New York Public Library.)

Stairway to the sealed entrance to the Ramble Cave. (Courtesy of Talbor Von Sregor, Atlas Obscura.)

The original 1865 Calvert Vaux and Jacob Wray Mould design for the Victorian folly Belvedere Castle, built in 1869.

Olmsted called the park *rus in urbe*, Latin for "the country in the city." It was also "night in day," an expression of silvery vanishments, and shadowy trysts of hidden glades glowing weirdly in a kind of narrative moonshine.

For paradise, now read "utopia." A secularization has occurred. The visions of the mystics are to be realized here and now in leaf and stone. But this practicality has not obliterated the yearning desire for the unknown place of authentic life. Today's Central Park nature walks and Euell Gibbons-inspired gathering expeditions are *echoes* of hunting-gathering culture and of the totemic spirituality of the borderland between clearing and forest. Central Park re-creates these longed-for images in the form of recreation. Because, of course, in fact Central Park is *not* paradise, *not* utopia, but rather the image or trace of utopia. Central Park is *not* the phalanstery, and the world has *not* been transformed into harmony.

Walter Benjamin used the concept of the "utopian trace" to explain the success of the commodity. Marx had pointed out that the commodity plays "metaphysical tricks." Benjamin attempted to produce an epistemology or even a theology by which to understand this metaphysics. In brief, we desire a commodity for the trace of something in it rather than for its actual value or use. We desire a memory or taste of an aura of authenticity and of life. The living tree or human, or the work of art in its unique immediacy, all possess this aura. In the reproduction of the image of this aura the commodity carries out its strange seduction: "your money for your life!" Or rather, for a promise of that authentic life, the real thing now, which the commodity will always postpone and put off, and never actually deliver. The mere trace of authentic life will induce us to hope that *next time*, our money *will* buy us happiness. Again we're disappointed, and again seduced. After all, no one agrees to work, consume, die in utter hopelessness. The commodity gives us hope even as it denies its realization. It reminds us of our buried utopian desires, perhaps only subliminally, our longing for a truer life. The more the commodity is reproduced, the more diluted and diminished its aura becomes. Advertising tries to restore a seductive image of aura, but if this image did not in some way assuage our loss, we would not buy it.

Seneca Village (Courtesy of the New York Historical Society.)

Benjamin performed an archeological dig for the remnants of aura and of desire in the sad and dusty junk shops of the Paris arcades. He searched out the remnants of a gift economy (to use Marcel Mauss's term) embedded within the structure of the commodity economy. He found *something*: imaginal vestiges fractaled into the body of spectacular alienation. Trace elements of an everyday life permeated and transformed by the marvelous, by happiness, which is never merely ordinary. He called this *something* the "utopian trace."

Is Central Park a commodity? In three meanings of the term, yes, certainly. First, to build the park, squatters had to be forcibly removed from the site. [*Here's a quote from a history.*]

A noxious element in the park was several squatter camps described as city suburbs, and according to official opinion, suburbs more filthy, squalid and disgusting can hardly be imagined. If the inhabitants were spared yellow fever, a newspaper observed, it would only be because Death himself hesitates to enter such a place. There, Indians, Blacks and Whites [*Note: Indians, Blacks and Whites.*] lived in hopelessness. As many as five thousand occupying caves, lean-tos and tin can shacks. They lived by pig farming, goat keeping, bone boiling, garbage picking and moonshining. Around their premises one observer said, 'The low ground was steeped in an overflow and mush of pig sties, slaughterhouses and bone boiling works, and the stench was sickening.' Coiners, poachers, sneak thieves and trollops were also present. Religious denominations sent missionaries there. The largest community, Seneca Village, was in from the West 80s. Charity-minded ladies built a church, All Angels Church, on the east side of Eighth

Avenue for these people. In the churchyard the squatters could bury their dead, until, the city, in 1851, in an ordinance aimed directly at them, forbade burials below 86th Street. When the city took title, it was judged, some hundred thousand cats, chickens, cows, dogs, geese, goats, pigs and horses belonging to the squatters roamed the site.

All Angels Episcopal Church, West 81st Street, whose original ministry was the Seneca Village settlement in what became Central Park.

In 1853, before Olmsted came on the scene, the new park patrol carried out a campaign of violence which had clear political overtones.

Action that year was limited to some ground clearing and a lengthy tussle to evict the squatters. For this last, the Central Park Police was formed, consisting of a captain, three sergeants and fifteen men. The battle was quickly joined. Falling back before the better discipline and armament of the lawmen, the squatters, with their greater knowledge of the terrain, waged stubborn guerrilla warfare with fusillades of bricks. Ultimately, after combat lasting weeks, they bowed to the inevitable, and retreated to the open spaces of Haarlem and Yorkville.

The Red, Black, White — probably Irish — mix of the squatters' settlement is typical of antebellum racial harmony amongst the marginal poor, concord which gave rise to all the tribes of tri-racial isolates in eastern America, despised by all other classes with eugenic vengeance. And why? Because they alone realized the true melting pot ideal of democracy, but only in rebellion against morality and work, against the emerging world of the commodity.

And who were those Indians? If this text were a piece of fiction, I would assert that they were the last of that Algonquin clan who sold Manhattan to the Dutch. [*Perhaps they were.*] Colonial New York City had been the scene of riots in 1741, in which the Red, Black, and Irish marginal poor were united to "kill Whites" as one of the *Irish* rioters put it. Central Park was in part the answer of the commodity class to this potential for social violence, or "anarchy," as it was called.

Point two. Central Park was bought and sold, it was commodified. New York City paid more for the land than the U.S.A. paid for all of Alaska a few years later. The city, in a sense, expected to make a profit on this capital through patronage. The fiscal history of the park has been a war between honest park-loving administrators and graft manipulators like the Tammany Democrats.

On the whole, and over the long *durée*, the park lovers have prevailed and in a sense extricated Central Park from the web of commodity relations, making it a privileged preserve, supported by the people outside capital forces, or to combat out of the struggle, as it were. Note: the public park is exempt from the rule of capital, in part because parks do not produce. But the garden city—Olmsted was also a pioneer in that field—was a similarly utopian idea that failed, precisely because it was not so exempt. The garden city is a park with houses, but it must interface with capital in order to fulfill its productive role. It's protected to a degree, but not privileged. Thus, garden cities either decay into slums, or else into enclaves of bourgeois self-embedding.

The park does not compete, it's the free space wherein class conflict undergoes reconciliation, or truce, or at least a cease-fire. Or at least, so it seemed until recently. If parks are finally deteriorating into the crime zones predicted by Olmsted's enemies, it's because parks are now competing to survive in a commodity world where the image of nature on a screen has been substituted for the image of nature as park, which in turn was originally a substitute for nature itself. Whatever that might be.

Calvert Vaux (1824-1895) (Courtesy Wikimedia Commons) and Frederick Law Olmsted (1822-1903). (Engraving by James Notman, Wikimedia Commons.)

Point three. But this situation of privilege which defines the word "park" as we now understand it, could only come about through the realization that nature cannot compete with capital. That the birds and bears can field no battalions nor corner any markets. And that the laissez-faire city is the space of disappearance of nature.

According to what we might call Michel Foucault's Law society only recognizes some abstraction such as nature or sexuality when it has in some way begun to vanish. Thus, the Romantics — and the Victorian American reformers are nothing if not Romantics — actually defined, or even created, nature, only when the Industrial Revolution had proclaimed the final triumph of man over wildness and wilderness. Nature is thus a spectacular reproduction of actual wildness or wilderness. Nature is now hypostasized in opposition to the unnatural. [*That is to say nature becomes a "thing in itself," a Kantian category, in opposition to the unnatural.*] The human world appears for the first time as *un*natural, totally *other* than nature. To bridge this split, again, to reproduce harmony then, becomes the goal of the reformers, the utopians, and the utopian socialists.

The park thus emerges as a commodification of the urge to bridge the gap between nature and civilization. The park will be, in effect, a spectacle of reconciliation, a spectacle that any city will buy if it wishes to appear civilized, according to Romantic standards, and these standards completely permeated 19th century America. Nature is displayed through the park, just as sadness is displayed through elaborate funereal

aesthetics, or progress is displayed through great world fairs and exhibitions, or morality is displayed through building churches and founding reform societies. Displayed as the commodity is displayed, now, for the first time in shop display windows. Iconized, or emblematized.

The earliest park builders had called themselves "improvers," and landscape architecture is not an oxymoron, but a metaphysical assertion of the role of art in reconciling the unnatural technology—the city—and the natural, on a higher level of synthesis. The park, in fact, is a Hegelian object. The park is meant to be an improvement, or a perfecting of both nature and culture, but one might argue that in reality it is only a packaging of the image of this perfectibility.

Of course the park can be condemned from the point of view of ideology, whether of Marxism or of Deep Ecology. The park is a kind of people's opium, or the park is an insult to the true spirit of wildness and wilderness, etc., etc.

But, I have not asserted the park's commodity aspect merely in order to damn the park. Like most New Yorkers I feel the city's parks have saved my sanity more than once. Especially Central Park, which really does express as a work of art something of that which body and soul receive from wilderness and wildness, precisely the effect Olmsted intended. It would be churlish to deny this successful quality of Central Park and emphasize only its recuperative or spectacular force. And precisely here, the concept of the utopian trace comes into play.

Willowdell Arch, Central Park, 23 September 1862. Standing on East Drive, near 67th Street, are, L-R: Andrew Green, treasurer and controller of the Central Park Board of Commissioners; George Waring, drainage engineer; Calvert Vaux, landscape architect; Ignaz Anton Pilat, landscape gardener; Jacob Wray Mould, associate landscape architect; and Fredrick Law Olmsted. (Courtesy of Rare Book Division, New York Public Library; photo by Victor Provost.)

Olmstead intended Central Park to contain more than just a trace of utopia. In fact, since "trace" also means trailway or path, we might say that Olmsted intended a whole network of such trails, a living map of utopian traces. If Central Park has commodity aspects, at least the commodity here is made up of actual living things with a genuine aura, like trees,

shrubs, water, animals, humans. Of course Central Park has been reproduced in similar parks in other towns, including Prospect Park, built in Brooklyn by Olmsted and Vaux. And, Central Park is engaged in reproduction, it reproduces the effect of nature for each visitor or customer. But, as a whole, Central Park displays far more aura than any mere technological construct manufactured to simulate the authentic and rob us of our hard-earned wages. And well it should, because it was not made by venal capitalist swine, but by great artists who were also utopian reformers.

Belvedere Castle on a busy winter day, the spires of the San Remo apartment building behind the gazebo. (Photo courtesy of Nicholas Santasier.)

A few years ago, some New York anarchists, looking for a place to hold a champagne picnic, decided to declare the Belvedere Tower a one day duration

Temporary Autonomous Zone. And so, they measured out a space on the tower's lawn with black balloons, and settled in for a fine June afternoon. Despite the fact that hundreds of people walked through their space in the course of the day, they achieved the autonomy they desired. Just as the celebrants of Be-Ins in the Sheep Meadow had achieved it in the 60's. And just as every family picnic or softball game or folk dance party or occult ritual or love affair can achieve autonomy in the park, provided they are carried on with due decorum and respect for others, something which comes *naturally* in the midst of Olmsted's masterpiece, where light and space induce and combine a sense of privacy and a sense of comradeship.

Central Park brings out the utopian element in most of its aficionados. If New Yorkers never agree on anything else, they're unanimous in protecting Central Park from the ravages of inhuman politicians. They keep shelling out money for its restoration, and form volunteer organizations to raise funding, or wield power to preserve Central Park more or less as Olmsted intended it. Not so much a refuge from reality, but a reminder that reality can be utopian.

Angel of the Waters at Bethesda Terrace, dedicated in 1873 and designed by Emma Stebbins. The base was designed by Calvert Vaux, with sculptural details by Jacob Wray Mould. The four cherubs embody Peace, Purity, Health and Temperance. It references both the healing Pool of Bethesda, located in the Muslim Quarter of Jerusalem, and the blessing of the Croton Aqueduct, opened in 1842, which brought New York City dependable clear water for the first time. (Photo by Benson Kua, courtesy of Creative Commons.)

www.ingramcontent.com/pod-product-compliance
Lightning Source LLC
Chambersburg PA
CBHW040744250626
47164CB00006BA/164